PRINCEWILL LAGANG

Healthy Boundaries, Healthy Relationship

First published by PRINCEWILL LAGANG 2023

Copyright © 2023 by Princewill Lagang

All rights reserved. No part of this publication may be reproduced, stored or transmitted in any form or by any means, electronic, mechanical, photocopying, recording, scanning, or otherwise without written permission from the publisher. It is illegal to copy this book, post it to a website, or distribute it by any other means without permission.

Princewill Lagang asserts the moral right to be identified as the author of this work.

First edition

This book was professionally typeset on Reedsy.
Find out more at reedsy.com

Contents

1	Introduction	1
2	Defining Boundaries	4
3	Self-Awareness and Boundaries	7
4	Establishing Personal Boundaries	10
5	Boundaries in Communication	13
6	Navigating Emotional Boundaries	17
7	Respectful Conflict Resolution	20
8	Balancing Individuality and Togetherness	23
9	Digital Boundaries in the Digital Age	26
10	Family and Social Boundaries	30
11	Revisiting and Adjusting Boundaries	33
12	Sustaining Healthy Boundaries	36

1

Introduction

In the realm of human interactions, relationships form the cornerstone of our social lives, influencing our emotions, decisions, and personal growth. At the heart of every successful relationship lies a concept often overlooked but indispensable: healthy boundaries. These invisible lines demarcate the limits of acceptable behavior, ensuring that individuals' autonomy, emotions, and well-being remain respected and safeguarded. In this chapter, we delve into the fundamental significance of healthy boundaries within relationships and explore how they intricately weave into the fabric of overall relationship well-being.

1.1 The Significance of Healthy Boundaries

As the old adage goes, "good fences make good neighbors," the notion of boundaries in relationships operates on a similar principle. Boundaries are not restrictive barriers; instead, they are vital tools that facilitate open communication, mutual understanding, and emotional safety. Just as a well-constructed fence sets clear property lines and expectations, establishing healthy boundaries delineates emotional and psychological spaces between individuals. This serves to prevent misunderstandings, conflicts, and the erosion of personal identities that can arise when these lines are blurred.

1.2 The Role of Boundaries in Relationship Well-being

The intricate dance of human connections flourishes when individuals recognize and honor each other's boundaries. Boundaries act as a framework for establishing consent, ensuring that both parties engage in interactions willingly and comfortably. When these boundaries are acknowledged, it creates an environment where trust and respect thrive, providing a fertile ground for empathy and intimacy to blossom.

Furthermore, healthy boundaries promote a balanced power dynamic within relationships. They empower individuals to voice their needs, desires, and limits without fear of reprisal or judgment. This empowerment fosters a sense of agency, bolstering self-esteem and contributing to overall emotional well-being.

In the absence of clear boundaries, relationships may traverse into uncomfortable territories, leading to emotional strain, resentment, and even toxicity. When personal limits are repeatedly ignored or violated, individuals might feel diminished, trapped, or taken advantage of, which can ultimately erode the foundation of the relationship.

1.3 Navigating the Journey Ahead

Throughout this exploration, we will delve deeper into the multifaceted nature of boundaries in relationships. We will examine various types of boundaries—emotional, physical, and intellectual—and the ways they manifest in different relationship dynamics. We will also uncover the challenges that can arise when establishing boundaries, from societal influences to personal insecurities.

As we progress, it is crucial to remember that setting and maintaining

INTRODUCTION

healthy boundaries is not a one-size-fits-all formula. Each relationship is unique, shaped by the individuals involved, their histories, and their shared experiences. Through our discussions, we aim to equip you with insights, strategies, and practical advice to navigate the delicate balance between asserting your autonomy and fostering meaningful connections.

In conclusion, healthy boundaries are the cornerstone of resilient and fulfilling relationships. By recognizing their significance and understanding their role in promoting emotional well-being, we embark on a journey to cultivate healthier, more authentic connections with others. As we turn the pages of this exploration, let us delve into the world of boundaries with curiosity and an open heart, ready to reshape our understanding of relationships and their transformative potential.

2

Defining Boundaries

2.1 Understanding the Essence of Boundaries

Before delving deeper into the intricacies of boundaries within relationships, it is essential to establish a clear understanding of what boundaries entail. At its core, a boundary is an invisible line that demarcates the distinction between one's personal space, emotions, thoughts, and the space of others. It represents the limits and guidelines that an individual sets to protect their well-being, identity, and autonomy while engaging in interactions with others.

Boundaries are not rigid barriers designed to keep people at a distance; rather, they are flexible and dynamic guidelines that foster healthy communication, respect, and connection. They help to establish a safe environment where individuals can express themselves authentically without the fear of being belittled or dismissed.

2.2 Types of Boundaries and Their Significance

Boundaries manifest in various forms within relationships, each playing a crucial role in maintaining a balanced and respectful interaction. Here, we explore three primary types of boundaries and their significance:

2.2.1 Physical Boundaries

Physical boundaries refer to the physical limits that individuals establish to safeguard their personal space and body. These boundaries can involve physical touch, personal belongings, and even the physical environment. Respecting physical boundaries means understanding and asking for consent before initiating any physical contact and recognizing that personal space differs for each individual.

2.2.2 Emotional Boundaries

Emotional boundaries pertain to the separation of one's emotions from those of others. They involve acknowledging one's own emotions, understanding their triggers, and being able to differentiate between one's feelings and those of others. Emotional boundaries prevent emotional enmeshment, where one person's emotions are excessively intertwined with another's, leading to confusion and potential emotional turmoil.

2.2.3 Intellectual Boundaries

Intellectual boundaries revolve around respecting an individual's thoughts, ideas, and beliefs. These boundaries allow individuals to engage in open and respectful discussions without feeling attacked or invalidated. Respecting intellectual boundaries involves actively listening, refraining from belittling differing viewpoints, and acknowledging that diversity of thought enriches conversations.

2.3 The Interplay of Boundary Types

While these boundary types might seem distinct, they often intersect and overlap within relationships. For instance, emotional boundaries might influence physical boundaries, as someone with strong emotional boundaries might be more inclined to set clear physical limits. Similarly, intellectual boundaries can impact emotional boundaries, as the respectful exchange of differing ideas can contribute to emotional well-being.

2.4 Balancing Flexibility and Firmness

The establishment and maintenance of boundaries require a delicate balance between flexibility and firmness. Boundaries should be adaptable to evolving circumstances, yet firm enough to uphold one's well-being and values. Striking this balance ensures that relationships remain respectful and dynamic, without becoming stagnant or encroaching on one another's personal space.

In the chapters that follow, we will delve into the nuances of setting and communicating boundaries effectively. By comprehending the different types of boundaries and their importance, we lay the groundwork for cultivating healthier, more harmonious relationships. Remember that boundaries are not barriers to connection but rather the scaffolding upon which genuine understanding and respect can flourish.

3

Self-Awareness and Boundaries

3.1 The Crucial Link Between Self-Awareness and Boundaries

In the intricate landscape of relationships, self-awareness serves as the compass that guides us in setting, maintaining, and respecting boundaries. Self-awareness involves a deep understanding of our emotions, values, needs, and limits. It is the foundation upon which we build the framework of healthy boundaries, allowing us to navigate interactions with authenticity and confidence.

3.2 Reflecting on Needs and Limits

Before embarking on the journey of defining boundaries, it is essential to take a pause and engage in honest introspection. Reflect on your emotional responses, triggers, and the moments when you felt your boundaries were tested. Consider what makes you feel comfortable, respected, and valued within relationships.

1. Identifying Emotional Responses: Pay attention to your emotional reactions in various situations. Are there instances when you feel uncomfortable,

anxious, or disrespected? These emotions can be indicators that a boundary has been crossed or is at risk of being crossed.

2. Understanding Triggers: Explore the sources of your emotional triggers. These triggers can stem from past experiences, trauma, or deeply ingrained beliefs. Recognizing these triggers empowers you to communicate your boundaries effectively and set limits where necessary.

3. Defining Needs: Consider your emotional and psychological needs within relationships. Do you require space for solitude? Do you value open communication? Identifying these needs allows you to communicate them clearly to others, fostering a deeper sense of understanding.

4. Recognizing Limits: Reflect on your limits—what you are willing to tolerate and what you are not. Boundaries are about safeguarding your well-being, so it's crucial to identify the actions or behaviors that you find unacceptable.

3.3 The Role of Communication

Self-awareness goes hand in hand with effective communication. Once you have gained insights into your emotions, needs, and limits, the next step is to articulate them to others. Clear and open communication is the bridge that allows individuals to establish boundaries, promote mutual understanding, and prevent conflicts.

3.4 Embracing Personal Growth

Engaging in self-awareness and boundary-setting is not a static process. It is a continuous journey of personal growth and self-discovery. As you navigate relationships and practice setting and respecting boundaries, you will likely encounter challenges and learn valuable lessons about yourself and others.

By nurturing self-awareness, you empower yourself to take charge of your emotional well-being and create healthier connections. Remember that setting boundaries is not a selfish act; it is an act of self-respect and an invitation for others to respect your individuality as well.

3.5 Exercises for Reflection

1. Emotional Journaling: Maintain a journal to jot down your emotional responses to various interactions. Reflect on what triggered these emotions and what boundary might have been involved.

2. Needs and Values Inventory: List your emotional and relational needs, along with your core values. This inventory will serve as a reference point when defining boundaries.

3. Boundary Visualization: Imagine yourself in scenarios where your boundaries might be challenged. Visualize how you would respond while maintaining your emotional well-being.

In the upcoming chapters, we will delve into the art of effective communication and strategies for navigating boundary-related conversations. As you embark on this journey of self-awareness and boundary-setting, keep in mind that it is a transformative process that empowers you to build relationships rooted in authenticity and mutual respect.

4

Establishing Personal Boundaries

4.1 Unveiling the Art of Setting Boundaries

Setting personal boundaries is an art that requires a combination of self-awareness, effective communication, and a commitment to one's well-being. In this chapter, we delve into practical strategies for identifying, communicating, and maintaining personal boundaries within relationships.

4.2 Strategies for Identifying Personal Boundaries

1. Reflect on Past Experiences: Consider instances from your past when you felt uncomfortable, disrespected, or taken advantage of. These situations can shed light on the boundaries that you need to establish.

2. Pay Attention to Emotional Reactions: Notice when you feel upset, anxious, or uneasy during interactions. These emotional responses can often be signals that your boundaries are being encroached upon.

3. Consult Your Values and Needs: Refer to the emotional and relational needs inventory you created. Align your boundaries with your core values

and the aspects that contribute to your well-being.

4.3 Communicating Boundaries Effectively

1. Be Clear and Specific: When communicating your boundaries, be precise about what behaviors or actions you find acceptable or unacceptable. Ambiguity can lead to misunderstandings.

2. Use "I" Statements: Frame your boundaries using "I" statements to express your feelings and needs without making the other person defensive. For example, say "I need some space to recharge" instead of "You're always invading my privacy."

3. Choose the Right Timing: Engage in boundary-setting conversations when both parties are calm and receptive. Avoid discussing boundaries during moments of tension or conflict.

4. Practice Active Listening: Encourage the other person to share their thoughts as well. Listening fosters understanding and demonstrates your commitment to open communication.

4.4 Benefits of Clear Communication

4.4.1 Prevention of Misunderstandings: Clear communication helps prevent assumptions and misinterpretations, ensuring that both parties are on the same page regarding expectations.

4.4.2 Fostering Mutual Respect: When you openly communicate your boundaries, you show respect for your own needs and values. This, in turn, encourages the other person to respect your boundaries as well.

4.4.3 Building Trust: Transparent communication builds trust within relationships. When others see that you are willing to express your limits, it creates a foundation of trustworthiness.

4.4.4 Enhancing Emotional Well-being: Establishing and communicating boundaries directly contributes to your emotional well-being. By addressing potential conflicts early on, you prevent the accumulation of negative emotions.

4.5 Maintaining and Reassessing Boundaries

Personal boundaries are not static; they may evolve over time as circumstances change. Continuously assess and adjust your boundaries based on your experiences, growth, and evolving needs. Regularly engaging in self-reflection ensures that your boundaries remain relevant and effective.

In the chapters to come, we will delve into navigating boundary-related challenges, such as handling pushback and managing guilt. By mastering the art of setting and communicating personal boundaries, you create a solid foundation for healthier, more respectful, and fulfilling relationships.

5

Boundaries in Communication

5.1 The Interplay of Boundaries and Communication

Effective communication is the cornerstone of successful relationships, and boundaries play a pivotal role in shaping how we engage in conversations. In this chapter, we delve into the intricate connection between boundaries and communication, along with techniques to foster respectful and productive dialogue.

5.2 Impact of Boundaries on Communication

Healthy boundaries lay the groundwork for open, honest, and respectful communication. When individuals establish and uphold their boundaries, it creates an environment where conversations can unfold without fear of judgment, manipulation, or breach of trust. Here are some ways boundaries influence communication:

1. Encouraging Vulnerability: When boundaries are respected, individuals feel safe sharing their thoughts, feelings, and vulnerabilities without the fear of them being used against them.

2. Promoting Active Listening: Clear boundaries ensure that both parties feel heard and understood. This encourages active listening, where each person genuinely engages with the other's perspective.

3. Preventing Miscommunication: Boundaries provide guidelines for communication, reducing the chances of misunderstandings or misinterpretations.

4. Facilitating Conflict Resolution: When individuals understand and respect each other's boundaries, conflicts can be addressed more constructively, leading to quicker resolutions.

5.3 Techniques for Respectful and Effective Conversations

5.3.1 Active Listening:

Active listening involves giving your full attention to the speaker, without interrupting or formulating your response prematurely. This technique fosters a sense of validation and helps the speaker feel heard and respected.

5.3.2 Reflective Responses:

After the speaker finishes, respond by paraphrasing their thoughts and feelings to confirm your understanding. This shows that you are actively engaged and interested in comprehending their perspective.

5.3.3 "I" Statements:

Express your thoughts and feelings using "I" statements, which focus on your emotions and experiences rather than making assumptions or accusations. For example, say "I felt hurt when…" instead of "You always…"

5.3.4 Setting Conversation Boundaries:

Explicitly state any boundaries related to the conversation. For instance, you can say, "Can we avoid discussing certain topics?" or "Let's focus on finding solutions rather than placing blame."

5.3.5 Asking Open-Ended Questions:

Encourage deeper discussions by asking open-ended questions that can't be answered with a simple yes or no. This invites the speaker to share more about their thoughts and feelings.

5.4 The Role of Non-Verbal Communication

Non-verbal cues such as body language, facial expressions, and tone of voice can significantly impact communication. Pay attention to your own non-verbal signals and those of the speaker to ensure that they align with the respectful and open atmosphere you aim to create.

5.5 Practicing Patience and Empathy

Effective communication requires patience and empathy. Understand that each individual's communication style and comfort level with boundaries might differ. Be patient in navigating conversations, and approach them with empathy to foster understanding even in challenging discussions.

5.6 Exercises for Practicing Boundaried Communication

1. Role Play: Engage in role-playing scenarios to practice setting and respecting boundaries during conversations.

2. Mindful Communication: Practice mindfulness during conversations, focusing on your responses and non-verbal cues to ensure they align with your communication boundaries.

3. Boundary Check-In: Periodically assess your comfort levels during conversations and reflect on whether your boundaries are being respected or compromised.

By integrating boundaries into your communication techniques, you pave the way for meaningful dialogues that contribute to relationship growth and harmony. In the next chapter, we'll delve into navigating difficult conversations and addressing conflicts while maintaining healthy boundaries.

6

Navigating Emotional Boundaries

6.1 The Significance of Emotional Autonomy

Emotions are a deeply personal aspect of our lives, shaping our perceptions, reactions, and connections. Within relationships, maintaining emotional autonomy is vital for fostering a healthy balance between personal well-being and shared experiences. In this chapter, we explore the importance of emotional boundaries and strategies for navigating them.

6.2 The Essence of Emotional Boundaries

Emotional boundaries involve recognizing and respecting the emotional space of both individuals within a relationship. They ensure that each person's feelings are acknowledged without becoming entangled or overwhelmed by the other's emotional state. Emotional boundaries are essential because they:

1. Preserve Individual Identities: Emotional boundaries prevent the merging of identities, allowing each person to maintain their unique emotional experiences and perspectives.

2. Prevent Emotional Drain: Without clear emotional boundaries, one person's emotional distress can easily transfer to the other, leading to emotional exhaustion and strain.

3. Foster Empathy: Emotional boundaries create an environment where empathy flourishes without the weight of absorbing another person's emotions.

6.3 Strategies for Supporting Each Other's Emotions

6.3.1 Active Listening and Validation:

When someone shares their emotions, practice active listening by giving them your full attention. Avoid rushing to offer solutions or advice. Instead, validate their feelings by acknowledging their emotions without judgment.

6.3.2 Offer Empathy, Not Absorption:

While it's natural to want to ease someone's pain, remember that you can support their emotions without fully absorbing them. Offer empathy by expressing understanding and care while maintaining your emotional distance.

6.3.3 Respect Requests for Space:

Sometimes, individuals need space to process their emotions independently. Respect their requests for solitude or time alone, understanding that this is a healthy way of managing emotions.

6.3.4 Communicate Your Boundaries:

Express your own emotional boundaries clearly and kindly. Let your partner know what kind of emotional support you can offer and when you might need space to manage your own feelings.

6.3.5 Practice Self-Care:

Prioritize self-care to ensure your emotional well-being. When you are emotionally grounded, you're better equipped to offer genuine support to others without becoming overwhelmed.

6.4 Recognizing Signs of Emotional Overload

It's important to be aware of signs that you might be becoming emotionally overwhelmed by someone else's feelings. These signs can include increased stress, irritability, and a sense of emotional heaviness. If you notice these signs, it's a cue to reassess your emotional boundaries and engage in self-care.

6.5 Exercises for Navigating Emotional Boundaries

1. Emotional Check-Ins: Regularly discuss emotional boundaries with your partner. Share what types of emotional support you each prefer and how you can respect each other's boundaries.

2. Journaling: Write about your emotional responses to various situations, exploring how you can maintain emotional autonomy while being supportive.

3. Empathy Practice: Engage in empathy exercises that allow you to understand and connect with someone's emotions without absorbing them.

By nurturing emotional autonomy and respecting emotional boundaries, you create an environment that supports both individual growth and mutual understanding within relationships. In the next chapter, we'll explore the complexities of physical boundaries and how they contribute to the overall health of relationships.

7

Respectful Conflict Resolution

7.1 The Role of Boundaries in Conflict Resolution

Conflict is an inevitable part of any relationship, and how we navigate it can significantly impact the dynamics between individuals. Boundaries play a vital role in conflict resolution by providing a framework for respectful and effective communication during disagreements. In this chapter, we explore how boundaries contribute to conflict resolution and the importance of maintaining respect even in the heat of the moment.

7.2 Establishing a Foundation of Respect

Respect serves as the cornerstone of healthy conflict resolution. When individuals have clear boundaries, they enter disagreements with the understanding that personal limits will be respected, even when opinions clash. This foundation of respect allows for open communication and collaboration, reducing the risk of arguments escalating into hurtful or damaging territory.

7.3 The Role of Boundaries in Conflict De-escalation

Boundaries help de-escalate conflicts by providing guidelines for engagement. When both parties know their emotional limits and triggers, they can communicate with greater care and avoid exacerbating the situation. By respecting each other's boundaries, conflicts are less likely to escalate into emotionally charged exchanges.

7.4 Staying Respectful During Disagreements

7.4.1 Active Listening:

During conflicts, practice active listening to ensure that both parties feel heard and valued. By focusing on understanding the other person's perspective, you create a foundation for a more constructive conversation.

7.4.2 Avoid Personal Attacks:

Maintain emotional boundaries by refraining from personal attacks, blame, or belittling language. Focus on addressing the issue at hand rather than attacking the person.

7.4.3 Take Breaks if Necessary:

If a disagreement becomes heated, it's okay to take a break to cool off. Communicate the need for a pause and set a specific time to reconvene the conversation.

7.4.4 Stick to the Issue:

Stay focused on the topic of disagreement and avoid bringing up unrelated past issues. This helps prevent conflicts from derailing and becoming more complicated.

7.4.5 Communicate Boundaries:

During a conflict, clearly communicate your emotional boundaries. Let the other person know if a particular topic or approach is making you uncomfortable, and request that they respect your boundaries as well.

7.5 Resolving Conflicts Through Compromise

Boundaries can guide compromise by helping individuals identify the areas where they are willing to be flexible and where they need to remain steadfast. When both parties respect each other's boundaries and are open to finding common ground, conflicts can be resolved in a way that honors everyone's needs and values.

7.6 Exercises for Respectful Conflict Resolution

1. Conflict Reflection: Reflect on past conflicts and analyze how respecting boundaries might have contributed to a more positive resolution.

2. Boundary-Centered Communication: Engage in a role-playing exercise where you practice resolving a conflict while clearly respecting each other's boundaries.

3. Conflict Resolution Journal: Maintain a journal to document your conflict resolution experiences, noting how boundary awareness influenced the outcomes.

By incorporating boundaries into conflict resolution, you create an environment where disagreements can be addressed constructively without causing harm to the relationship. In the final chapter, we'll summarize key takeaways and provide a roadmap for applying the principles of boundary-setting to build healthier relationships.

8

Balancing Individuality and Togetherness

8.1 The Duality of Relationships: Individuality and Togetherness

The dance between maintaining individuality and fostering togetherness is a delicate yet essential aspect of every relationship. Nurturing personal growth while cultivating a sense of connection requires a nuanced understanding of boundaries. In this chapter, we delve into the intricacies of this duality and how healthy boundaries contribute to striking the right balance.

8.2 The Challenge of Maintaining Self within a Relationship

When individuals enter into relationships, they often navigate the challenge of retaining their sense of self amidst the shared experiences. While connection is essential, losing oneself in the relationship can lead to a loss of identity and autonomy. This is where boundaries play a pivotal role.

8.3 The Role of Healthy Boundaries

Healthy boundaries provide a framework for embracing both individuality and togetherness. By setting clear emotional, physical, and intellectual boundaries, individuals can engage in relationships without compromising their personal growth and well-being.

8.4 Supporting Individual Growth

8.4.1 Space for Pursuits: Healthy boundaries allow space for pursuing individual interests and goals. Each person has the freedom to explore passions, hobbies, and personal development without feeling suffocated by the relationship.

8.4.2 Emotional Autonomy: Maintaining emotional boundaries ensures that individuals have the autonomy to process their emotions, seek self-discovery, and grow independently.

8.4.3 Nurturing Self-Care: Setting boundaries for self-care establishes a foundation of well-being that contributes to personal growth. This, in turn, enriches the relationship by bringing a fulfilled and self-aware individual to the partnership.

8.5 Cultivating Mutual Connection

8.5.1 Respect for Individuality: Healthy boundaries involve respecting each other's individual needs, desires, and identities. This respect fosters a sense of trust and authenticity within the relationship.

8.5.2 Open Communication: Boundaries encourage open and honest communication about personal needs and boundaries. This dialogue strengthens the connection by creating an atmosphere of understanding and compromise.

8.5.3 Collaboration: Setting and respecting boundaries often involves collaboration, which enhances the partnership's sense of equality and shared responsibility.

8.6 Striking the Balance

Balancing individuality and togetherness requires ongoing awareness and communication. It's a dynamic process that evolves as individuals and the relationship itself grow and change.

8.7 Exercises for Balancing Individuality and Togetherness

1. Personal Visioning: Reflect on your individual goals and aspirations. Share these with your partner and discuss how you can support each other's personal growth.

2. Boundary Negotiation: Engage in a conversation with your partner about boundaries that will enable both of you to maintain your sense of self while strengthening the relationship.

3. Relationship Check-In: Regularly assess how well you're maintaining a balance between individuality and togetherness. Discuss any adjustments that might be needed.

Incorporating healthy boundaries into your relationship journey empowers you to embrace your individuality while nurturing a meaningful and harmonious connection. As you apply the principles of boundary-setting, you'll find yourself navigating relationships with greater authenticity, respect, and emotional well-being.

9

Digital Boundaries in the Digital Age

9.1 The Digital Landscape of Relationships

In the modern era, technology has woven itself intricately into the fabric of our lives, including our relationships. While digital connectivity offers numerous benefits, it also presents unique challenges when it comes to maintaining healthy boundaries. This chapter explores the impact of technology on relationships and strategies for navigating the digital world while preserving privacy and connection.

9.2 The Paradox of Connectivity

While technology has enabled unprecedented levels of communication, it has also blurred the lines between personal and public spheres. As a result, individuals often find themselves struggling to establish and maintain boundaries in the digital realm.

9.3 The Impact on Relationships and Boundaries

9.3.1 Privacy Concerns: The digital age has given rise to privacy concerns, as personal information becomes easily accessible. Establishing boundaries around what you share online is crucial for protecting your identity and well-being.

9.3.2 Constant Connectivity: The expectation of constant availability can strain relationships. Setting boundaries around response times and establishing "tech-free" zones or times can help maintain balance.

9.3.3 Digital Etiquette: The lack of non-verbal cues in digital communication can lead to misunderstandings. Clear boundaries around respectful communication, avoiding heated discussions online, and using emoticons to convey emotions can mitigate this.

9.4 Strategies for Maintaining Digital Boundaries

9.4.1 Establishing Social Media Boundaries:

Define what you're comfortable sharing on social media platforms. Consider limiting who can view your posts and reviewing your friend or follower list periodically.

9.4.2 Setting Communication Boundaries:

Establish clear expectations with your contacts regarding response times to messages. Communicate when you'll be offline and unable to respond promptly.

9.4.3 Tech-Free Zones/Times:

Designate specific areas or times where technology is off-limits, allowing for undistracted personal interactions and quality time.

9.4.4 Unplugging Rituals:

Create rituals to unplug from technology regularly, such as a "screen-free hour" before bed or a dedicated "digital detox" day each month.

9.4.5 Cybersecurity Awareness:

Educate yourself about online security and privacy measures to ensure your personal data remains protected.

9.5 Fostering Connection in a Digital World

9.5.1 Quality Over Quantity: Focus on the quality of interactions rather than the quantity. Meaningful conversations can occur even in brief exchanges.

9.5.2 Virtual Presence: Be fully present during digital interactions. Engage actively and attentively to strengthen the sense of connection.

9.5.3 Digital Date Nights: Plan intentional digital interactions with loved ones, such as virtual movie nights or online games, to maintain a sense of togetherness.

9.6 The Power of Digital Detox

Regularly disconnecting from technology allows for rejuvenation and reconnection with the offline world. Embrace periods of digital detox to recalibrate your relationship with technology and prioritize real-world experiences.

9.7 Exercises for Navigating Digital Boundaries

1. Digital Inventory: Assess your online presence and consider what information you're comfortable sharing. Make necessary adjustments to your privacy settings.

2. Boundary Audit: Reflect on your digital interactions and evaluate whether

you've been maintaining healthy boundaries. Adjust your habits if needed.

3. Tech-Free Day: Designate a day where you minimize or eliminate your digital engagement, focusing on real-world interactions and activities.

By setting and maintaining digital boundaries, you can harness the benefits of technology while safeguarding your well-being and the quality of your relationships. In the concluding chapter, we'll recap key takeaways and offer a comprehensive guide for applying the principles of boundary-setting to enhance various aspects of your life.

10

Family and Social Boundaries

10.1 The Impact of External Influences

Relationships exist within a broader context that includes family, friends, and social circles. These external influences can both enrich and complicate relationships, making it essential to establish boundaries that maintain the integrity of the partnership. In this chapter, we explore the influence of family and friends on relationship boundaries and offer strategies for setting and maintaining healthy boundaries with external factors.

10.2 Navigating Family Dynamics

Family relationships carry a significant emotional weight, and their impact on personal boundaries can be profound. While families provide a support network, they can also introduce challenges when it comes to respecting the boundaries of a romantic partnership.

10.3 Strategies for Setting Family Boundaries

10.3.1 Open Communication: Have open and honest conversations with your family about the boundaries you're establishing in your romantic relationship. Explain your reasons and ask for their understanding and support.

10.3.2 Defining Roles: Clearly define the roles of family members in your relationship. Establish which decisions are meant to be made within the partnership and which ones involve external input.

10.3.3 Prioritizing Partnership: Communicate to your family that your romantic relationship is a priority. This doesn't mean neglecting them, but rather setting clear boundaries to ensure a balanced approach.

10.4 Nurturing Friendships While in a Relationship

Friendships are an essential part of life, but they can also affect the boundaries within a romantic partnership. It's important to maintain friendships while ensuring they enhance, rather than compromise, the primary relationship.

10.5 Strategies for Setting Social Boundaries

10.5.1 Balance and Inclusion: Find a balance between spending time with friends and nurturing your romantic relationship. Ensure that your social circle supports your partnership and respects your boundaries.

10.5.2 Communication with Friends: Communicate with your friends about your relationship boundaries. Ask for their support and understanding, while also acknowledging that your priorities have shifted.

10.5.3 Joint Social Activities: Engage in joint social activities that involve both your partner and your friends. This fosters integration and allows everyone to interact comfortably.

10.6 Responding to External Pressure

External influences can sometimes challenge established boundaries. It's important to stand firm in your boundaries while respectfully addressing any external pressure or opinions that might arise.

10.7 Exercises for Establishing Family and Social Boundaries

1. Family Boundaries Discussion: Initiate a conversation with your partner about how to establish healthy boundaries with family members while maintaining a supportive relationship.

2. Friendship Assessment: Reflect on your friendships and assess if they align with your relationship boundaries. Consider whether any adjustments are needed.

3. Boundary Communication: Practice communicating your boundaries with friends or family members, explaining why these boundaries are important for your relationship's well-being.

By navigating family and social boundaries, you create a space where your partnership can thrive while still engaging with the significant people in your life. As we conclude this guide, let's recap the key principles of boundary-setting and offer a comprehensive roadmap for applying them to enhance various aspects of your relationships and overall well-being.

11

Revisiting and Adjusting Boundaries

11.1 The Dynamic Nature of Boundaries

As relationships evolve, so do the dynamics and needs of individuals involved. Boundaries that were once effective may require adjustments to accommodate personal growth, changing circumstances, and the evolving nature of the partnership. In this chapter, we delve into the dynamic aspect of boundaries and the significance of open communication when revisiting and adjusting them.

11.2 The Role of Growth and Change

Personal growth is a constant journey, and relationships are vehicles for that growth. As individuals evolve, their boundaries might shift to reflect new priorities, interests, and insights. Similarly, changes in external circumstances, such as moving, career changes, or family dynamics, can also impact boundary needs.

11.3 Why Revisit and Adjust Boundaries?

11.3.1 Reflecting on Changes: Regularly revisiting boundaries allows individuals to recognize how they've evolved and assess whether their current boundaries align with their growth.

11.3.2 Addressing Challenges: When conflicts arise due to boundary clashes, it's an opportunity to reevaluate and adjust boundaries to prevent similar issues in the future.

11.3.3 Nurturing Connection: Adjusting boundaries can deepen the connection within a relationship, as both parties actively engage in understanding each other's changing needs.

11.4 The Role of Open Communication

11.4.1 Honesty and Vulnerability: Open communication is the cornerstone of boundary adjustments. Share your changing needs, emotions, and perspectives with honesty and vulnerability.

11.4.2 Active Listening: Encourage your partner to express their thoughts and feelings about potential boundary adjustments. Actively listen and validate their perspective.

11.4.3 Mutual Decision-Making: Collaboratively decide on boundary adjustments that honor both individuals' needs and aspirations. This shared decision-making process fosters mutual respect.

11.5 Strategies for Revisiting and Adjusting Boundaries

11.5.1 Scheduled Check-Ins: Set aside regular times to discuss the state of your relationship and the effectiveness of your current boundaries. This prevents issues from accumulating.

11.5.2 Acknowledging Milestones: Mark significant milestones, such as anniversaries or personal achievements, by reflecting on the journey and considering whether boundary adjustments are needed.

11.5.3 Seeking Professional Guidance: In complex situations, seeking the assistance of a relationship counselor or therapist can provide valuable insights and guidance in navigating boundary adjustments.

11.6 Exercises for Revisiting and Adjusting Boundaries

1. Individual Reflection: Spend time individually reflecting on how you've grown and what aspects of your boundaries might need adjustment.

2. Mutual Visioning: Engage in a conversation with your partner about your collective vision for the relationship's future and how boundary adjustments can support that vision.

3. Boundary Audit: Regularly review your boundaries and assess whether they are still relevant and effective. Adjust as necessary.

As you navigate the journey of revisiting and adjusting boundaries, remember that flexibility, open communication, and mutual understanding are key. By embracing the dynamic nature of relationships and proactively adapting your boundaries, you create a foundation for growth, connection, and mutual respect that can enrich every aspect of your life.

12

Sustaining Healthy Boundaries

12.1 Reflecting on Your Boundary Journey

As you come to the conclusion of this guide, it's a valuable moment to reflect on the journey you've embarked upon to establish and maintain healthy boundaries. You've explored the nuances of setting boundaries, understood their role in various aspects of relationships, and learned strategies for navigating challenges. Now, let's distill the key takeaways and offer guidance for sustaining these boundaries over time.

12.2 Key Takeaways

12.2.1 Self-Awareness: The foundation of healthy boundaries lies in self-awareness. Understand your emotions, needs, and limits to effectively communicate your boundaries.

12.2.2 Clear Communication: Open and respectful communication is vital for setting, adjusting, and maintaining boundaries. Use "I" statements and active listening to foster understanding.

12.2.3 Empathy and Respect: Respecting others' boundaries while expecting them to respect yours creates an environment of empathy and mutual respect within relationships.

12.2.4 Flexibility: Recognize that boundaries can evolve over time due to personal growth and changing circumstances. Be open to revisiting and adjusting them as needed.

12.2.5 Self-Care: Prioritize your emotional and mental well-being by setting boundaries that protect your energy and preserve your personal space.

12.2.6 Continuous Learning: Boundaries are a lifelong practice. Stay curious, learn from your experiences, and refine your boundary-setting skills.

12.3 Sustaining Healthy Boundaries

12.3.1 Regular Check-Ins: Schedule periodic check-ins with yourself and your partner to assess the state of your boundaries and ensure they remain aligned with your evolving needs.

12.3.2 Self-Reflection: Continuously reflect on your emotional responses, triggers, and the effectiveness of your boundaries. Adjust them as you gain deeper insights.

12.3.3 Mindful Communication: Maintain a mindful approach to communication, being aware of how your words and actions impact others' boundaries.

12.3.4 Practice Gratitude: Express gratitude for the mutual understanding and respect that boundaries bring to your relationships. Celebrate the positive impact they have.

12.3.5 Seek Support: If you encounter challenges or uncertainties, don't hesitate to seek guidance from trusted friends, family members, or professionals.

12.4 A Roadmap for Boundary Sustainability

12.4.1 Revisit This Guide: Periodically revisit this guide to refresh your understanding of boundary-setting principles and to find inspiration for maintaining healthy boundaries.

12.4.2 Journaling: Maintain a boundary journal where you record insights, experiences, and reflections related to your boundary journey.

12.4.3 Accountability Partner: Share your commitment to sustaining boundaries with a trusted friend or partner who can offer support and hold you accountable.

12.4.4 Celebrate Progress: Celebrate your achievements in maintaining boundaries. Recognize the positive impact they have on your well-being and relationships.

12.5 Your Journey Ahead

As you move forward, remember that the journey of sustaining healthy boundaries is a continuous and rewarding process. The skills you've honed through this guide will serve as a compass in navigating the complexities of relationships, personal growth, and meaningful connections. By nurturing your self-awareness, empathy, and communication skills, you're equipped to create a life enriched by healthy boundaries that promote authenticity, well-being, and lasting connections.

www.ingramcontent.com/pod-product-compliance
Lightning Source LLC
LaVergne TN
LVHW010439070526
838199LV00066B/6091